Painting the Southwest

by Ladislao Gutierrez

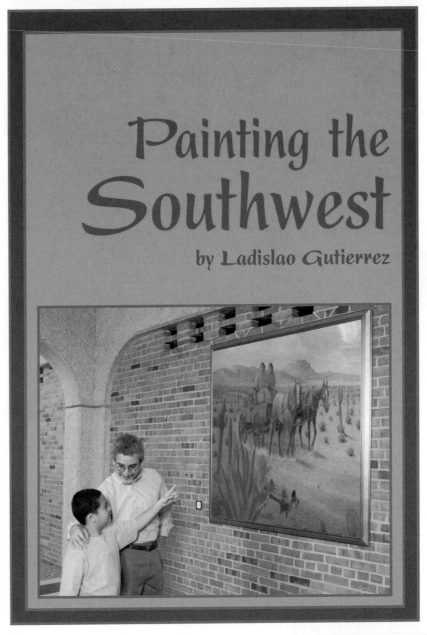

PEARSON

Glenview, Illinois • Boston, Massachusetts • Chandler, Arizona
Upper Saddle River, New Jersey

art gallery

painting

My grandfather is an artist. He lives in Skull Valley, Arizona. I visit him from New Jersey every summer. Grandpa takes me to art galleries. An art gallery is a building or a room used to show paintings and sculptures, or statues and other carved art. We talk about the paintings. Grandpa tells me about the artists and the oil paints, pens, pencils, watercolors, and other materials artists use.

Grandpa tells me, "Every artist has something to say. An artist talks to us through paintings and sculptures. Artists share their ideas and feelings in their art."

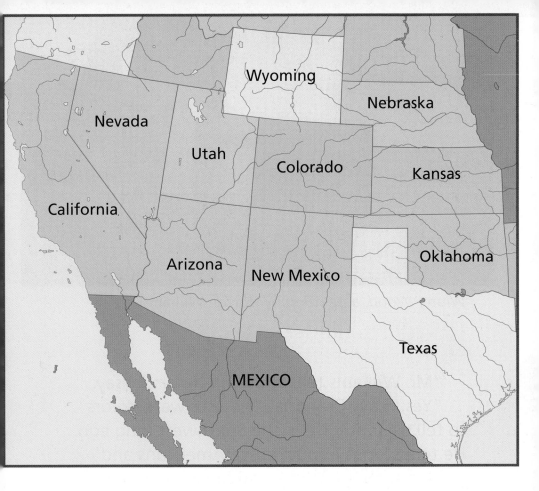

I want to be an artist when I grow up.

Today, we are looking at watercolors by Norton Williams. Mr. Williams lived in California and the Southwest in the 1900s. For many years, he was a painter for the United States Navy.

When Mr. Williams grew older, he moved to Arizona. He saw cowboys and Native Americans. He saw small pueblos and ranches. He spent time in the desert. He used watercolors and pastels to paint the people and places of the American Southwest.

---

pueblos: Native American villages of the Southwest

Winter Wood, a painting by Norton Williams

"Mr. Williams tells stories in his art," I say.

"Yes," says Grandpa. "He uses watercolors to tell us about life in the Southwest long ago. He tells stories about Native Americans and cowboys, about burros and horses, and about pioneers and ranchers."

I look closely at a painting. "That looks like snow on the ground. I thought the Southwest was all desert."

Grandpa laughs. "It can snow in the desert. A desert is just a place with very little rain. It isn't all sand and cactus. Up in the mountains, there is high desert. You can have tall pine trees in the high desert. You can even have snow up there."

We look at the next painting. I ask Grandpa, "What's that behind the woman? It looks like a city."

"Some native people lived in cities. Some didn't." says Grandpa. "There were cities all over the Southwest. Some of the old cities were big, but most were small pueblos. Some cities or pueblos were built on the tops of cliffs, or into mountainsides."

A Stroll with the Twins, by Norton Williams

Next, we look at a watercolor of an old town. The people in it look Hispanic, like the people in my family.

"The next folks to come to the Southwest were Hispanic," says Grandpa. "The Southwest used to be part of Mexico. Now California, Arizona, New Mexico, Texas, and other states are part of the United States. We Mexican Americans still live here."

Grandpa and I like this painting a lot.

Hispanic: from Spain or Latin America

South of the Border

Grandpa explains, "The Mexican people built villages or towns too. Some people lived in town. Others rode in to the towns on horses or in wagons. Those people didn't go to town very often.

"Back then, people made almost everything they needed at home. They went to town to buy things they couldn't make, such as tools and saddles for their horses. Some people went to church and to the bank in town too."

I look closely at the painting. "The woman probably bought her bucket in town," I tell Grandpa. "I bet the girl bought her umbrella there too."

Extend Language   Cognates

Sometimes a word in one language sounds or looks like a word in another language. If these words have similar meanings, they are called *cognates*. Cognates can help you learn a new language. Here are some English-Spanish cognates. Can you name others?

English	Spanish
bank	banco
desert	desierto
mountain	montaña

A painting of cowboys is next. I know all about cowboys. Many cowboys came to the Southwest to drive cattle to market. They kept the cattle in big groups or in long lines to go across the land. That was called a "cattle drive."

Cowboys called the land where the cattle grazed, or ate grass, "the range." Sometimes the land was a prairie or plains where grasses grew. Sometimes the land was a desert of sand and cacti and not much grass.

Grandpa points to the wagon in the painting. A cook kept his pots and pans and all his cooking tools in it. When the cowboys stopped for the night, he could cook them a meal. He could cook anywhere.

---

market: a place to buy and sell things

Beans and Coffee

Heading in

I look at another painting. "Those cowboys are in the middle of nowhere!" I say to Grandpa. Cowboys were out on the range a lot. They didn't see many people until they got their cattle to market.

"Yes," says Grandpa. "I think cowboys liked to have a lot of land around them. Even now, parts of the Southwest don't have very many people."

Grandpa lives far from other people too. I think many of the people in the Southwest still like having lots of land around them.

The truck shakes as we drive across a dry riverbed. I say, "Things were softer long ago. Weren't they, Grandpa?" Grandpa looks at me and asks what I mean. I explain, "Mr. Williams used soft colors in all his paintings. I think he wanted us to know that times were soft too. They were gentle."

Grandpa smiles. "The people worked hard in those days, just as we do today. Life was hard back then. But I know what you mean. Life was full of chores, but it was different. People spent more time at home and in nature."

"That's why Mr. Williams didn't use many bright or very dark colors," I decide. "He showed us a quiet time."

---

chores: tasks, jobs   **in nature:** outdoors

Back at Grandpa's house, I watch him paint. Grandpa is painting a picture of his own house. He uses oil paints. Oil paints are thick. Grandpa paints with bright colors. Grandpa paints a lively, colorful sunset.

"I liked Mr. Williams's paintings," I say. "But I like the way you paint too!"

"Every artist has a special style," Grandpa says. "I wonder how you will paint one day."

"I do, too," I reply. "I do, too!"